HOW TO STAY STRESSE...

...D

HOW TO STAY

STRESSED

Written by DOUGLAS STEWART
Illustrated by MINA YAMASHITA

If there has
ever been a flood
worse than Noah's,
it has to be the
flood of so-called
self-help material on
"stress management"
and "burnout." Magazines,
newspapers, talk-shows,
TV specials, video tapes, seminars,
nation-wide surveys, weekend retreats,
theatrical productions, mental health
pamphlets, psychiatric counseling, computer
programs –

everything short of . . .

the 82nd Airborne –

has

been thrown into

the battle against

stress and burnout.

Niagara looks like an anemic trickle

compared to the deluge

of stress management books.

How do I know? I've been there.

I'm a Stress Management Veteran.
I've been involved with every one of the above,
plus a few we don't discuss in front of the
children.

Has this well-intentioned monsoon of facts, figures, and horror stories done any good? Well, look at the people around you. Do you know anyone who is less stressed today than they were, say, five years ago?

I doubt it.

Do I think the debilitating effects of stress, tension, and burnout are any less severe a problem for you today than they ever were?

No!

Am I tired of swimming upstream, telling you things about stress management you don't want to hear – shouting in the burnout wilderness?

Yes!

Therefore, I will no longer fly in the face of the obvious. Nor will I waste your valuable time trying to contradict what should by now be apparent to anyone with a grain of sense.

Most of you out there
WANT to stay stressed!

Ok, maybe that's a little extreme.

But how else to explain that despite this veritable torrent of stress management information, very few of you have significantly changed your life-styles? How to explain that most job situations seem even more stressful now than they were ten years ago? Or that stress-related illness, if anything, seems to be on the increase?

In short, if so many of you are apparently choosing to stay stressed, then you must be finding some advantages to your choice. After all, it's just basic human nature to choose the behaviors that give us the greatest payoffs. Any jelly-smeared six-year old can tell you that. If you choose to ignore the wealth of advice on how to lower excessive stress and tension while improving health and performance . . . well, who am I to buck a trend? "If you want to be a leader, son," Uncle Albert, our family's perpetual politician, used to say, "find a parade and get in front of it."

So, as a recognized Stress Management Veteran, I'm going to help you become even better at what you obviously want to do:

. . . stay stressed!

THINKING ABOUT IT

Let's face it, no one who is the least bit creative need ever lack causes for being excessively stressed. Nor is there any lack of debilitating stress symptoms with which the guilt-ridden can punish themselves. No, at this point in the 20th Century, when it comes to stress and its symptoms, scarcity is definitely not our problem.

Here – take this little stress self-assessment and see for yourself:

THE *"Oh, Great, Another Test"* STRESS TEST

DIRECTIONS: Quickly mark those items that apply to you. Use a large crayon, #4 pencil, or a crow quill pen dipped in . . . well, suit yourself. There is no time limit.

❏ 1. You've become very negative about everything. "Sarcasm" is now your middle name.

❏ 2. You're starting to put down, avoid or bad-mouth things that were once important to you.

❏ 3. There are "Oh m'god!" changes in your sexual interest or abilities.

❏ 4. You feel trapped – rocks and hard places are your constant personal geography.

❏ 5. You wreck your social support system, turning off those closest to you.

❏ 6. Your physical health ain't what it used to be.

❏ 7. You're developing weird changes in your sleep and/or eating habits.

❏ 8. You're starting to believe that "Nothing can be done," that your problems are out of control, that it may be 911 Time.

SCORING

6 - 8 *Excellent!* You're doing a terrific job! Just don't listen to any of those bran-loving health missionaries who may want you to change your stressful ways. They're just jealous of the attention you're sure to get from the medical profession!

3 - 5 **OK**, but you must try harder! You're now only at the discomfort level. Real distress still lies ahead. Discover more stressors. Get your friends to help – most of us have a few who can point the way to total disaster.

1 - 2 **Woefully inadequate!** People will think you're not taking this Staying Stressed thing seriously enough! Put time aside every day to work on it. No pain, no gain. Patience, perseverance, and practice will get you to any stress level your underworked heart desires.

13

There, what did I tell you? Despite a lot of whimpering Do-gooders' efforts to the contrary, there still remains a more than adequate supply of knock 'em-dead stress symptoms. Enough, I estimate, to go around about seven times over. Sort of like nuclear weapons.

But no human activity occurs without some sort of reward or benefit. It may be conscious or unconscious, but it's there if you look deep enough. From years of personal experience, I contend that there are big payoffs awaiting you for Staying Stressed. Just follow along here:

Staying Stressed makes you Look Important.

Anyone as obviously stressed as you are must be working very hard, and is therefore Important & Worthwhile. Maybe even valuable to your company. You can't keep up the pace all the way to retirement, of course, but it really makes a terrific impression on people now. You can always slow down, perhaps permanently, later.

Staying Stressed lets you Avoid Intimacy.

I mean, anyone exhibiting even a few choice burnout symptoms certainly can't be expected to form close emotional ties. At least not healthy ones. Frankly, as a Burnout, you probably won't be much fun to be around anyway, let alone be close to emotionally. Works better than garlic, bad breath, or the wrong deodorant for keeping people at a distance.  Helps you avoid all the emotional hassles for which intimate relationships are justifiably notorious. If you don't believe me, just spend an afternoon with The Soaps. Compared to the hazards and pitfalls of intimate relationships, burnout is a piece of cake.

Trust me.

Staying Stressed helps you Avoid Responsibilities.

In the first place, when you're sufficiently stressed any nincompoop can see that you're obviously in no condition to be given any additional work.

15

The only thing you need more of is pity. Second, you're stressed enough that you don't have time or energy to be bothered with the unimportant stuff – someone else should take care of it. This gets you off the hook for such mundane chores as reports, lengthy meetings, lawn mowing, housecleaning, and, if appropriate, parenting.

Staying Stressed gives you a Chemical Rush.

I'll let you in on a well-kept secret, known only to select health care professionals, an occasional M.D., and most CEOs – stress is the cheapest drug on the street! Really! Since your adrenalin, the "stress hormone," is chemically similar to amphetamines, you can give yourself a hit any time you wish. Just get things stirred up with your family, co-workers, boss, or Significant Other, and you're flyin'. Do it often enough and you may be able to get yourself addicted to your own adrenalin. Then the people around you are in for all sorts of fun.

Staying Stressed gets you Pity.

After all, if you're blatantly over-stressed, people are bound to feel sorry for you, right? Come to your rescue? Bail you out of your miseries? That way, you don't have to make any efforts to change your behavior on your own. If you're persistent, you may not even have to take charge of your own life. And don't be concerned about using up your sympathy bank account with all the would-be Rescuers in your life. According to Barnum, there's one born every minute.

Staying Stressed helps you successfully avoid Success.

Why risk being "successful?" It only means more responsibility, bigger jobs, higher expectations, changed lifestyle, riskier decisions, people to manage, larger investments to hassle you. Doesn't make sense, does it? Good old comfortable Failures never have those problems. Simply by staying stressed, you can avoid the rat race. Let stress keep your performance level low enough and Success will never threaten you.

Or, if you're accidentally already on the verge of Success, staying stressed can keep you from really making it Big. Let the Jog-Every-Morning Set go for the gold.

Staying Stressed lets you use an Authoritarian Management/Parenting style.

NOW!

Most management experts agree that the authoritarian style – "Don't ask questions, Pat, just do as I say!" – may be justified under crisis conditions. Therefore, if you are a manager or parent who can keep everything around you in crisis and turmoil, you are justified in using an authoritarian style, right? No one in their right mind, or who has read the experts, would dare question that – or you. If pressed, just remind them how well it worked for Attila the Hun.

DOING IT

Many people, finally aware of what a good thing Staying Stressed can be, have asked me how to go about getting started on a Stress Maintenance Program right away.

Fortunately, there are a number of clinically-proven methods for staying stressed that have worked for literally tens of thousands of people just like yourself. These thoroughly-tested methods fall into three basic categories:

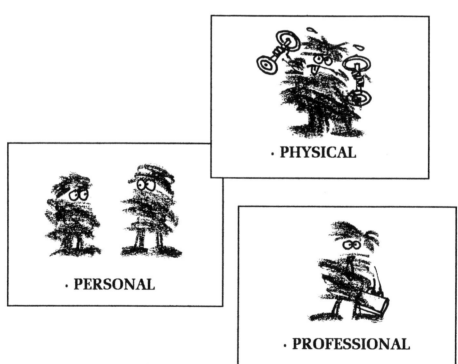

· PHYSICAL

· PERSONAL

· PROFESSIONAL

To ensure a completely successful stress maintenance program, you will want to concentrate on all
three areas simultaneously.

■ PHYSICAL

This is where you can make real progress
towards Staying Stressed with a minimum investment
of your precious time and effort.

Don't exercise.

Exercise does nothing but tone up your muscles,
improve your cardiovascular system – one of the best
targets for stress in men – relax your body, and change
your brain chemistry to provide a natural 'high.' Not
only that, it wastes time.

Better to spend that time on stress-building
activities and save yourself big bucks on running
shoes and cutesy exercise outfits. Aerobics classes
are just a strenuous way to blatantly show off nubile
young bodies that don't need exercise anyway.

Eat anything you want.

Ignore what the Doom-sayers claim about excessive cholesterol, fats, sugar, salt, vitamins, fiber, and red meat. They're all just trying to make names for themselves, get on TV talk shows and make a buck. It probably doesn't apply to you, anyway.

If you want to stay stressed right on through to the end of your workday, don't eat breakfast! Avoid it like the plague it is. Breakfast is only for kids, wimps, and over-the-hill athletes trying to make a comeback on cereal boxes. If you must have something, give your stress level a jump-start by picking up coffee and a couple of jelly doughnuts on the way to work. This will also gives you a good excuse in court for driving with your elbows.

Another thing: Stay out of health food stores, those expensive traps for the faddist fringe. Your body knows best, right? Give it what it craves. If cigarette smoke can't clean out your system, 28 flavors of yogurt isn't about to.

Stay overweight.

A European friend once told me after visiting the United States that we seemed to have a remarkable number of "pregnant men." Perfect! To get the maximum effect of stress on your body – especially your heart – stay at least 15% over your recommended weight. If you males out there can look down and see beyond your belt buckles, you're not really dead serious about this thing.

And you women, why should you be judged by those emaciated fashion models' standards? Face it, if Calvin Klein had wanted you to model jeans, you'd have heard from him by now.

Take in plenty of stimulants.

The Old Standards will usually do the job –
Caffeine, Nicotine, Sugar, Cola, Alcohol, Chocolate.
You know, all the things that make life really worthwhile. A help-yourself smorgasbord of these essentials
every day will get the job done nicely. They kick in a
mini-stress response which gets your adrenalin flow-
ing. And we already know how much fun that is!

And don't worry if morning coffee isn't your
thing. Just do what so many of your fellow Americans
do – have a couple of colas to get the day started. If
you're not certain that your current stimulant intake

is sufficient to Stay Stressed, try alternating days with and without your favorites for a week. That simple test will tell you if you need to increase your dosage to achieve the desired results – staying high-voltage wired.

And if the Old Standards have lost their punch, I'm sure there is someone in your neighborhood who can put you onto something
even more exotic.
Just cruise the malls.

Avoid pseudo-religious "woo-woo" practices.

Ignore the extravagant claims and improbable research suggesting that such far-Eastern relaxation imports as meditation, yoga, deep breathing, mental imaging, positive affirmations, or solar hot tubs can do anything positive for your mental or physical health.

No, the Protestant Work Ethic should be good enough for anyone, Protestant or not. If you want to stay stressed, stay out of hot tubs. Limit your oriental imports to the likes of cars, cameras, and VCRs. Our international trade deficit is frightening enough already.

■ PERSONAL

Here are a few of my recommendations from the Personal domain, every one a stress-producing classic:

Neglect your friends, family & lovers.

The mounting evidence that a strong social support system improves your physical health, psychological well-being, and probable life-span should immediately put you on your guard. In fact, there is a vicious rumor making the rounds that even a bad marriage is better than no marriage at all when it comes to lengthening your lifespan. That's sheer nonsense! Anyone who's ever been in a bad marriage can tell you that life just seems longer.

So don't call your friends,
   let them call you.

Let people around you know, in no un-certain terms, that your career comes first and friendships a distant second, if you have time – and you never have time. If a few stubborn people persist in trying to be your friend, don't take chances – insult them.

As for you men, don't emulate some females of our species, who are on the phone to friends at the first sign of trouble with any-thing from bedroom to boardroom. If we were supposed to use the phone that much, we'd have been born with a telephone jack in our navel. The fact that females live an average of seven years longer than we do is pure coincidence.

Besides, isn't that why
men invented life insurance?

Take negative criticism personally.

Now we're really into the nitty-gritty of an effective stress maintenance program. No matter how much people deny any personal intent behind negative feedback, don't believe them! Anyone who gives you negative feedback on your work, your ancestors, your dog, your house, your car – anything – is mounting a personal attack on you and should be treated accordingly.

Don't waste your valuable time trying to listen objectively or asking questions to clarify their meaning – be offended! Take umbrage, and take it pronto. Any wimp can accept feedback objectively, so prove you're a cut above the crowd and get upset! Return the attack! Get personal! Do it with enough fervor and you'll short-circuit any further problems with feedback. Once you've burned them a couple of times, those busy-bodies will leave you alone.

Stifle your sense of humor.

Take your choice: enjoy your sense of humor, or enjoy staying stressed. There's no room for both. Humor gives you distance from your problems, making a creative solution dangerously more likely. Laughing is even rumored to have positive healing effects on your body. Believe me, Staying Stressed is no laughing matter, and it shouldn't be treated as one. If humor was that good for us, Mark Twain would still be alive.

Be macho.

This is for males and females alike – there's no room for sexism when it comes to creative stress maintenance. (Save sexism to keep your co-workers in their place.)

How do you stay macho, short of leather jackets, naughty tattoos, and a big, bad Harley? Nothing to it! Just follow "The Grandmother's Adage." It contributes to more stress-related coronaries than any other advice in the English language:

"Remember, Dear, If You Want It Done Right,
Do It Yourself!"

In fact, just to be safe, have *that* tattooed on some private part of your body where you can look at it daily.

A useful corollary to Be Macho is *Don't share your problems with **anybody!*** Keep your dirty linen at home where it belongs. Sharing your problems with others not only risks lightening your own stress burden, it also encourages others to do the same with you – and you obviously have enough on your mind already. The exception – and, frankly, it's a judgment call – is if you think listening to someone else's problems will increase your own stress load. In that case, go for it!

Talk to yourself in the negative.

If you're like most of us, you seldom think about what you think about. Actually, if you listen in, you're talking to yourself most of the time. Don't be embarrassed. Even most sane people do it. The trouble is, many people waste this golden opportunity to raise their stress level.

If you'd like to add this valuable tool to your Staying Stressed maintenance program, practice delivering a few of these choice phrases to yourself at critical moments:

[You're in a socially embarrassing situation.]

"This is terrible! It will probably be in all the papers tomorrow – with *pictures*. No one will ever invite me anywhere in this town again! I just want to sink through the floor and die."

[You make a mistake at work.]

[You lose a competitive event.*]

"I'm such a klutz, such a loser. I was a fool to even agree to play in the first place. I always do everything wrong. I can never win at anything. The future looks hopeless. I wish I were dead!

*For example, a ping-pong match
with your niece, age 9.

35

See how easy it is? You're creative! I'm sure you can think up even better phrases of your own. Some people call this Catastrophic Thinking. There's really nothing like it for raising your stress level to even greater heights.

Practice it daily.

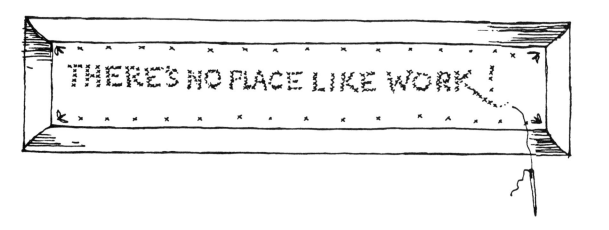

■ PROFESSIONAL

Now here's where the stress rubber hits the road – in your workplace. You spend at least a third of your waking hours here. (More, many more, if you're truly serious about achieving burnout.) It's your responsibility to take full advantage of the rich and abundant opportunities at work to increase your stress level. If experience teaches us anything about staying flat-out stressed, the workplace is the arena in which to do it. Remember, if God hadn't wanted us to stay stressed, there wouldn't be Corporations.

Here are a few methods that have proven themselves stressful ever since the first CEO called a Next Millennium's Budget Meeting in a cave:

Become a workaholic.

This one is so obvious that I'm embarrassed to even mention it! This is Staying Stressed 101 . . . kindergarten stuff. But I know there remain a few of you out there – a renegade handful – who still haven't tasted the joys of true Workaholism.

And it's not as hard to master as you may have been led to believe. In fact, it's so simple any fool can do it. Just put Work in front of everything else. Make it your new religion, and worship faithfully. For starters, if you have even the slightest doubt about your job performance, work *harder*, not *smarter*.

Always take work home evenings and weekends.

The more, the better. Don't concern yourself if you don't get to it. Do you think all those other brief-cases in the parking lot or getting off the 6:11 train ever get opened? Of course not! In fact, far better for your stress program if you ignore it – the resultant guilt can help raise your anxiety level to new highs.

Avoid vacations.

Keep reminding yourself that vacations are for school kids, confirmed bureaucrats, or unemployed actors. If your family forces you to take one every few years anyway, feel guilty and nervous the entire time you're gone.

Take work, a portable computer, and a cellular phone with you, just in case you develop insomnia or have to wait in line at a public restroom. Also, call your office frequently. Preferably every hour. Isn't that why they put pay phones in the Grand Canyon?

If you find you're starting to relax despite your best efforts to maintain a respectable stress level, think of this: *What if no one at work misses you?* That ought to keep the worry chemistry up to speed – for a couple of weeks, anyway. And any vacation longer than that is both indecently un-American and probably subject to close scrutiny by the IRS.

Think of yourself as Ms./Mr. Indispensable.

This is another aid to successful Workaholism, thus avoiding the expense and boredom of vacations. Convince yourself that you are Absolutely Indispensable. If you're in doubt about this, drop everything and perform this simple experiment:

The Never-Fail
Absolutely Indispensable Test[1]

1. Fill a 1-liter beaker with lukewarm water.
2. Remove all jewelry from your right index finger.
3. Insert the index finger into the lukewarm water.
4. Hold finger in the water for a *minimum* of 14 seconds.
5. Abruptly remove the finger from the water, carefully observing the results.

If a finger-sized hole remains in the beaker of water, you are Absolutely Indispensable.

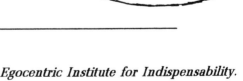

To summarize this important topic, successful Workaholism boils down to a simple matter of making sure there is no balance in your life between work and other rewarding activities. It's difficult for even the most dedicated among us to stay stressed if we're wasting time relaxing or otherwise restoring ourselves. Constant vigilance is the key. Practice reciting the Workaholic's Creed:

"A Job Well Done Is Never Enough, There Is Always More To Do"

GONE TO LUNCH !
~will call you in a week or so...

Don't waste time
        on time management.

You can successfully put a lot more pressure on yourself – and those around you – if you'll just follow faithfully these three simple rules of Stressful Time Management:

43

Do the little things first.

Start small. Don't tire yourself early in the game. Get at the Big Things whenever you get a chance – if ever. You'll worry a lot more if big things remain undone, and serious worry really gives the old stress level a terrific boost. Besides, if they're really important and you ignore them long enough, someone else will probably do them. And then you'll have even more to worry about.

Don't make lists.

Do projects in whatever order feels good. Don't pay attention to the importance other people attach to projects. That's their problem, not yours. They're just trying to give you busywork. Keep firmly in mind that prioritizing is the opiate of bureaucrats and other powerless functionaries.

Be constantly available
to everyone.

No matter what else you have to do, drop every-thing if someone wants your attention. Saying "No" might cause them not to like you anymore. Let their priorities run your day. Setting your own priorities eases conflict and confrontations, ruining an other-wise stressful day.

Not only that, trying to keep your own priorities straight tires the mind.

Also be meek, humble and passive in meeting your own time needs. Surrender your time to anyone more aggressive than you are. Remember that no less than Holy Scriptures promise that the meek shall inherit the Earth. You wouldn't want to screw things up and miss out on your legitimate inheritance, would you?

Besides, that smoldering volcano of resentment in your belly should keep the stress juices bubbling all day and, hopefully, into the night.

If those little time management gems don't sufficiently raise your stress level, try scheduling more things every day than you can possibly get done. That way, you never run the risk of feeling a sense of accomplishment. Believe me, nothing is more detrimental to your stress maintenance program than letting your guard down and feeling good about yourself. Sometimes even a minor slip – believing a silly compliment, for example – can wreck an otherwise wonderfully stressful morning.

Don't set personal or career goals.

If you're foolish or naive enough to set goals, you run the very real risk of putting your job and personal situations into a manageable perspective. Much less stressful, I'm afraid, than my recommended Serendipity Approach:

"What will be, will be."

Has a nice philosophical ring to it, doesn't it? It also ensures that you'll feel powerless most of the time, tossed about on the Sea of Life by an uncaring Fate, never to know the next hostile reef you'll be cast upon. Now that's not only Great Drama, it's also magnificently stressful!

Practice creative procrastination.

There's certainly no good adrenalin rush from getting things done early! Try what I call "Perils of Pauline Management": put everything off until the last minute, then dash in and rescue it. Just in the nick! You and your FAX machine saved the day! That really gets the old system pumped up. Yours and everybody else's. What a favor you've done everyone around you! Too bad not all of them are sufficiently grateful.

Besides, haven't you always said
you work better under pressure?
Don't change now and make
a liar of yourself.

Worry about things you can't control.

Let's be frank about serious worrying. Unless you count yourself among the independently wealthy, I'm sure you lead a busy worklife. Good, high quality worrying time is hard to come by, right? So don't waste it on the mundane, the manageables in your life. Instead, use your worrying time wisely.

49

Worry about instant-replay refereeing in the Super Bowl, ozone conditions over Antarctica, the Fall Fashions, is Elvis really dead – you know, the Big Issues.

In short, there's just no staying stressed sense in worrying about things you can control. The first thing you know, in a weak moment you'll be tempted to do something about it. And then where would your stress level be?

Constantly change things.

And not just a few things, either. Change everything you can – as often as possible. Don't let anyone become complacent as to what you'll do next. Keep 'em on their toes.

Remember that stress thrives on capricious change like crows on sweetcorn. Take advantage of it! Don't put off changes until they're actually needed and planned for – make them now! Keep things stirred up. Not only does this prevent your life from getting boring, it's also a great way to take others down The Primrose Path to Burnout with you.

And in case of The Ultimate Burnout, you do want friends who will attend your services, don't you?

ROCK

HARD
PLACE

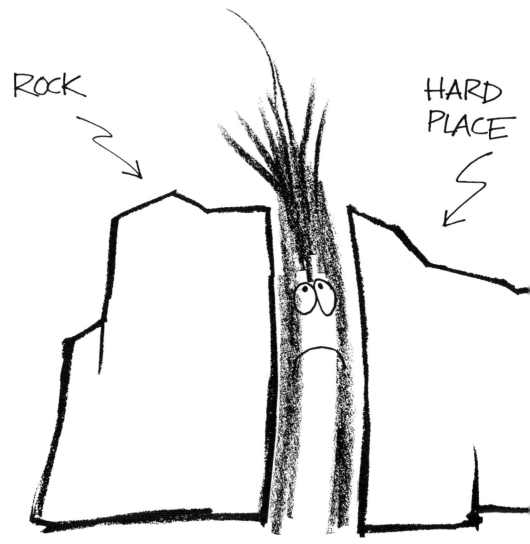

Get between "A Rock and A Hard Place."

Any fool can get along in a supportive work environment, with understanding managers and motivated employees. No challenge in that. Not much stress value, either. Far better for staying highly stressed to find a job where your managers or supervisors consistently give you responsibilities without the authority necessary to carry them out. Wonderful! One of the best! Don't mention it, though –

they might stop.

Exaggerate your skills and abilities.

When you're hired,
really stretch the truth –
you want this job,
don't you?

Now you can worry
the rest of the time
you're here that
you'll be found out.
Great! Gives you
a nice anxiety
base on which
to build your
on-the-job stress
maintenance
program. Nothing
like getting in
over your head
to raise the
panic level.

54

Work for an organization whose business practices violate your personal ethics or sense of fair play.

This can quickly turn even the most relaxing job into a real stress-producer. Maybe some fly-by–nighter making napalm baby formula for use in The Third World. Or driving a truck for the midnight disposal of radioactive waste in public parks. Use your imagination – there are opportunities every-where these days.

If all else fails, have an Office Affair.

No, not just some innocent little Fling in the storeroom during the Christmas Party, or an almost harmless rainy weekend in the Catskills. Oh, no, have a Really Messy One. Trash a few lives, wreck a few homes. Including yours, of course. Go public. Make sure that by the time you're finished, no one in town will hire you.

And if the these methods still aren't enough to raise you to stress levels approaching earth orbit – perhaps you're cursed with a stubbornly resilient metabolism – try this never-failed, yet last resort, procedure:

The A-B-C Last Resort Method

Step A. **Become a Total Perfectionist.**

Use any methods at your command. At this stage of the game, Friend, the end justifies the means.

Step B. **Set impossibly high personal standards.**

Go for SuperMom/SuperDad, The Best/Fastest Richest/Sexiest. Be perfect! Settle for nothing less. Don't let anything stand in your way of meeting those standards – family, friends, funerals. *Anything.*

Step C. **Beat up on yourself.**

When you can't meet these elevated standards, feel guilty, depressed, discouraged, inadequate and really down on yourself. Get nasty. After all, where your self-concept is concerned, you're the Expert. You know how to beat up on yourself better than anyone since the neighborhood bully.

That ought to do the trick. In fact, The A-B-C Method comes with a full Performance Guarantee: 5 years of migraines, or 50,000 asthma attacks, whichever comes first. Aren't you glad you didn't buy the first stress management book you ever saw? You could be out of Warranty by now.

Finally, keep working! Regardless of how stressed you're feeling, despite how your job performance is suffering, no matter what your co-workers are saying,

keep working!

You're on a roll! This is what Staying Stressed is all about! Go with the flow! Ignore the symptoms. The pains will go away. They're probably just indigestion, anyway. Be brave, have courage – you're approaching Burnout Nirvana. You've worked so hard to get here. Don't quit now!

And if the next face you see is that of a Paramedic, you'll know you've arrived.

POST SCRIPT

Oh, one other thing I should probably mention: Don't tell your Significant Other about our little Staying Stressed discussion. Research indicates that a high percentage of them disapprove of the stressful behaviors of their partners.

This obviously biased and narrow-minded attitude can have a very dampening effect on your entire Staying Stressed program.

Despite the insurance money, I suppose they're upset by the thought of all those elderly years alone in the Sun Belt.

That's it. Thanks for your attention.

**Good luck and
STAY STRESSED!**

59

DOUGLAS STEWART is an instructional play-wright, speaker, and management consultant.
Author of *Keeping the Fire Alive* and *The Power of People Skills,* he works with organizations in the areas of lowering stress, managing change, and team development. He keeps alive his fantasy of a base-ball career in "the Bigs" as a performance consultant to the Montreal Expos.

MINA YAMASHITA is an award-winning artist and graphic designer whose works run the gamut – from illustration to hand-bound artist's books, from pastel paintings to a line of hand-tufted rugs. Her illustrations are published nationally.
  Illustrator of *The Power of People Skills*, this is her second collaboration with Douglas Stewart.

Celebrate
Staying
Stressed

For Bulk Orders Call: 1-800/223-6397

Call in, Fax, E-Mail or Mail this Form

High Mountain Press Retail Sales
2530 Camino Entrada
Santa Fe, NM 87505-4835 USA

1-800/223-6397
Fax +1 505/471-4424
E-Mail: ORDERS@BOOKSTOR.HMP.COM

QTY	TITLE	PRICE
	Staying Stressed T-Shirt	$14.95
	Staying Stressed Coffee Mug	$7.95
	Staying Stressed Baseball Cap	$8.95

SUBTOTAL...

New Mexico Delivery Address Only Add 6.125% Tax
Handling: (All Others)_____ #Items x $2.50 Handling Each _____

GIFT SERVICES
_____ # Gift Wrap x $5.00 Each
_____ #Gift Certificate Amount + $3.00 each   _____

SHIPPING (SELECT ONE)
☐ Use my Courier: _____
   Account Number: _____
   Speed of Service: _____
☐ US 48 States Ground Shipping-
   10 Business days $3.00
☐ Second day - 2 days $9.00   _____
☐ Overnight - Next day $12.00
☐ Alaska, Puerto Rico, Hawaii: 5-7 days $12.00
☐ Canada Shipping: 2-3 days $15.00
☐ Europe•Australia • New Zealand
   • Mexico • Caribbean • Japan
   • Pacific Rim Shipping: 3-5 days $22.00   _____
☐ All other Areas shipping: 5-7 days $45.00
☐ All other Areas Weight Surcharge:
_____ # of pounds x $2.50 Shipping

TOTAL...

Name: _____
Company: _____
Street: _____
City, State: _____
ZIP, Postal Code: _____
Phone: _____
E-Mail Address: _____

PAYMENT METHOD
☐ Check or Money Order Enclosed
(Must be $US & drawn on a US, Canadian, or Euro Check bank account)
☐ MC   ☐ VISA   ☐ Amex   Exp. Date _____

Card Number: _____

Signature: _____

INW RD PRESS™

TITLES

For Bulk Orders Call: 1-800/223-6397

Call in, Fax, E-Mail or Mail this Form

High Mountain Press Retail Sales
2530 Camino Entrada
Santa Fe, NM 87505-4835 USA

1-800/223-6397
Fax +1 505/471-4424

Wholesale & Retail

US Trade Markets
Van Nostrand Reinhold
115 Fifth Avenue
New York, NY 10003
1/800-842-3636
Fax 606/525-7778

Canadian Markets
Nelson Canada
1120 Birchmount Road
Scarborough, Ontario M1K
5G4, CANADA
1-800-/268-2222 x444
Local 416/752-9100
Fax 416/752-8101

Asia, Pacific, and Hawaii
*International Thomson Publishing
Asia*
38 Kim Tian Road, #01-05
Kim Tian Plaza
Singapore 0316
Local 2-272-6497
Fax 2-272-6498

Japan
International Thomson Publishing
Kyowa Building   3rd Floor
2-2-1 Hirakawacho Chiyoda-Ku
Tokyo 102 JAPAN
Local +81-33-221-1385
Fax +81-33-237-1459

**Europe, Middle East, Africa,
South America,**
International Thomson Publishing
Berkshire House
168-173 High Holborn
London WC1V 7AA, UK
Local 44-71-497-1422
Fax 44-71-497-1426

**Australia and New Zealand
Markets**
Thomas Nelson Australia
102 Dodds Street
South Melbourne, 3205
Victoria, AUSTRALIA
Local 61 3 685-4111
Fax 61 3 685-4199

**Latin America,
Puerto Rico**
International Thomson Publishing
20 Park Plaza
Boston, MA 02116 USA
Local +1 617-423-4210
Fax +1 617-423-4325
London WC1V 7AA, UK
Local 44-71-497-1422
Fax 44-71-497-1426

QTY	TITLE	PRICE
	Oriental Medicine Resource Guide	$29.95
	Chinese Herbalist's Handbook	$29.95
	How to Stay Stressed	$9.95

SUBTOTAL...

New Mexico Delivery Address Only Add 6.125% Tax
Handling: (All Others): #Books x $2.50 Handling Each   _____

GIFT SERVICES
_____ # Gift Wrap x $5.00 Each
_____ #Gift Certificate Amount + $3.00 each   _____

SHIPPING (SELECT ONE)
☐ Use my Courier: _____
   Account Number: _____
   Speed of Service: _____
☐ US 48 States Ground Shipping-
   10 Business days $3.00
☐ Second day - 2 days $9.00
☐ Overnight - Next day $12.00
☐ Alaska, Puerto Rico, Hawaii: 5-7 days $12.00
☐ Canada Shipping: 2-3 days $15.00
☐ Europe•Australia • New Zealand • Mexico • Caribbean-
   • Japan • Pacific Rim Shipping: 3-5 days $22.00
☐ All other Areas shipping: 5-7 days $45.00
☐ All other Areas Weight Surcharge:__# of pounds x $2.50

TOTAL...

Name: _____
Company: _____
Street: _____
City, State: _____
ZIP, Postal Code: _____
Phone: _____
E-Mail Address: _____

PAYMENT METHOD
☐ Check or Money Order Enclosed (Must be $US & drawn on a US, Canadian, or Euro Check bank account)
☐ MC   ☐ VISA   ☐ Amex   Exp. Date _____

Card Number: _____
Signature: _____